ROBOT
The Mechanical Monster

ROBOT
The Mechanical Monster

David Annan

BOUNTY BOOKS
NEW YORK

Printed in the U.K. by
W. & J. Mackay Ltd., Chatham

Designers: Dave Allen and Graham Bingham
Cover design by Robert Ellis

(Frontispiece).
Talos threatens *Jason and the Argonauts* in the film version of 1963, animated by Ray Harryhausen.

Contents

Acknowledgements

We wish to give our thanks in the preparation of this book to RKO, 20th Century Fox, Paramount, MGM, Columbia-Warner and Joy Smith, United Artists, Allied Artists, First National, Universal, EMI and Mike Buist and John Fraser, Fox-Rank and Barbara de Law, British Lion, Davidson-Dallings, Hammer Films, Cinema International Corporation and Denis Michael, the British Film Institute stills department, the Cinema Bookshop, the Museum of Modern Art, Al Reuter, Brian McIlmail, Martin Jones, Walt Lee, Jerry Fiore and many others.

Man-made man

'I saw the hideous phantasm of a man stretched out, and then, on the working of some powerful engine, show signs of life, and stir with an uneasy, half vital motion. Frightful it must be; for supremely frightful would be the effect of any human endeavour to mock the stupendous mechanism of the Creator of the world.'

So Mary Shelley saw in 1816 the nightmare of Count Frankenstein creating his monster in his laboratory. She was about to create the legend of a new machine-made being, which would become one of the most powerful figures in mass fantasy. She was building on a tradition older than the Greeks and on an early vision of the universe, which seemed to her to work like a clock made by a Great Artificer. If man played at God, he could create life itself out of his ingenious machines.

Mechanical men had fascinated the Greeks. Hephaestus, the lame god of fire and the arts, was meant to have made the first robot, the bronze giant Talos. It was given to King Minos and set to guard the shores of Crete. Any stranger who landed on the island was clutched by Talos in a red-hot embrace. The one weakness of the metal giant was a stopper, which kept the vital conducting fluid flowing in the veins. When the Argonauts landed and Talos appeared, Medea managed to charm out the stopper, so that the liquid ran out and the giant fell down at their feet.

Hephaestus had other robots to help him in his heavenly laboratory — mechanical golden maidens, who served his guests and assisted at his experiments, forerunners of the false Maria in Lang's *Metropolis*. Willing robot

The robot Maria is created by Rotwang in Lang's *Metropolis* (1926).

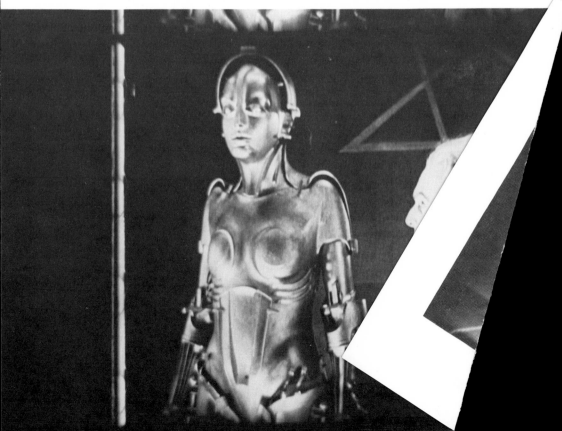

Rotwang makes his robot into flesh by electrodes plugged into a replica girl.

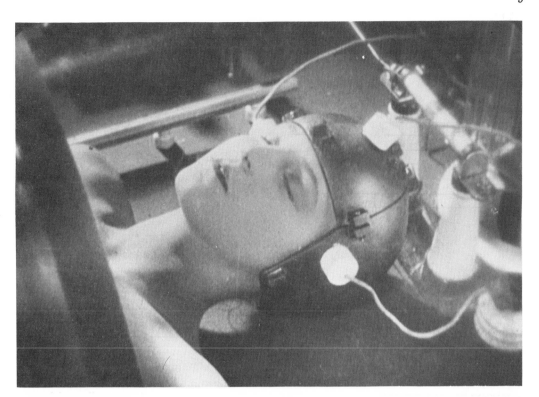

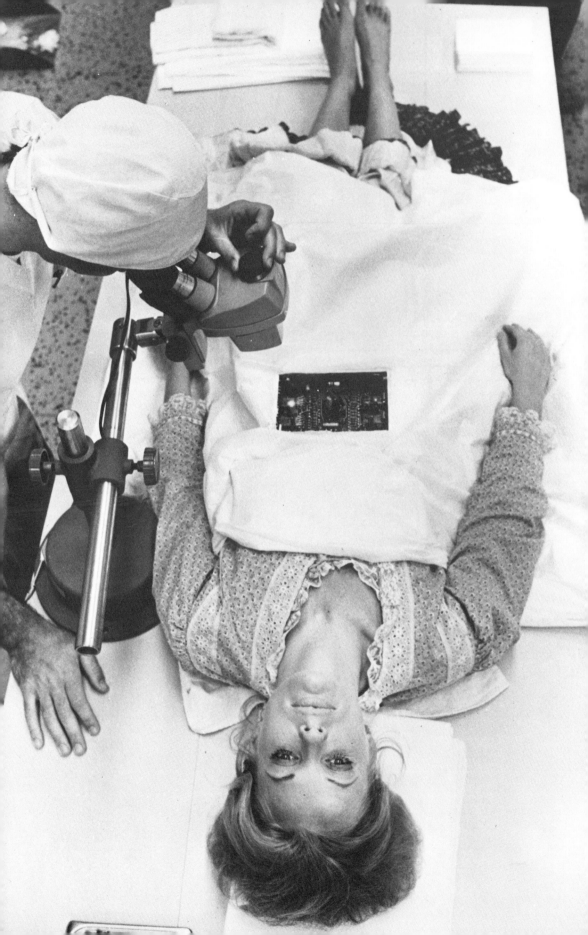

Vincent Price plays a modern Hephaestus with his killer robot maidens in Corman's *Dr. G and the Bikini Machine* (1965).

dolls have remained a strong male fantasy. The lame god was also ingenious, trapping his wife Aphrodite with her lover Mars in a wire net concealed above her bed, and surprising his mother Hera in the arms of a golden chair until she gave him what he wanted.

Hephaestus was the divine version of Prometheus, who stole both fire and the arts from heaven and took them down to men. It was no accident that the subtitle of Mary Shelley's Frankenstein was *The Modern Prometheus;* the myth had long fascinated her husband, Percy Bysshe Shelley. According to ancient belief, Prometheus had stolen fire from the Gods and had given it as a gift to mankind, which was slowly freezing to death. For his sin, he was condemned to be bound to a rock in the Caucasus and have his liver torn out eternally by an eagle. In other versions of the legend, Prometheus was

In *Westworld* (1974), a mini-computer plugs in the girl to serve the desires of the holiday-makers.

also the creator of mankind out of clay, and thus the inspirer of the fabled Rabbi Loëw, who made the clay monster, the Golem. Mary Shelley knew of the Golem from her collection of ghost stories called *Phantasmagoriana.*

Other sources lay behind the creation of Frankenstein's monster. The fact that it was given its vital spark by electricity (as well as the first part of its name) came from the contemporary experiments of Benjamin Franklin with sparks and lightning. Mary Shelley had also probably heard of the tales of Hoffman, which were written at the same time. In one tale, there was a mechanical dancing man, who could dance his partners to death. In another tale, there was a robot doll called Olympia, who was loved by a madman. The making of artificial life was a current topic.

Left: Rabbi Loew and his assistant try to hold up their clay monster in *The Golem* (1920). *Above:* The Golem wonders whether to kill or accept the trust of the little girl.

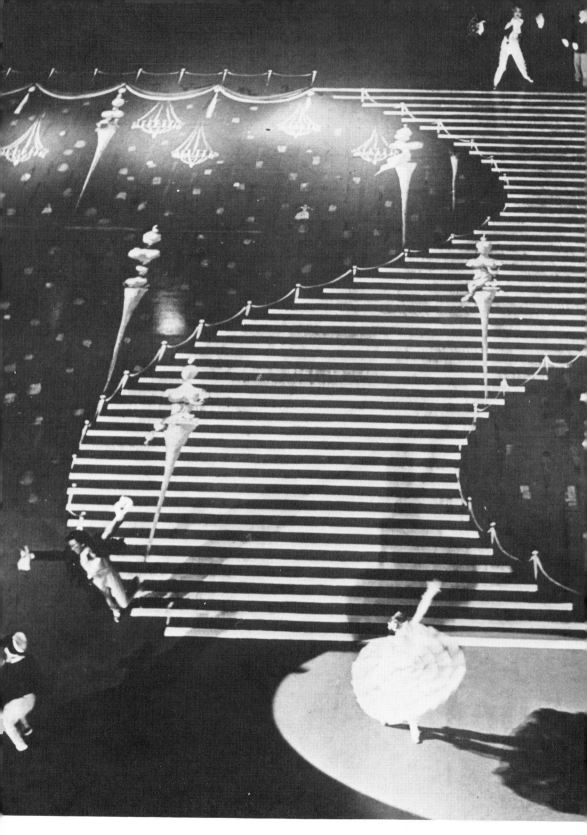

The mechanical doll Olympia dances on and on in *The Tales of Hoffman* (1951).

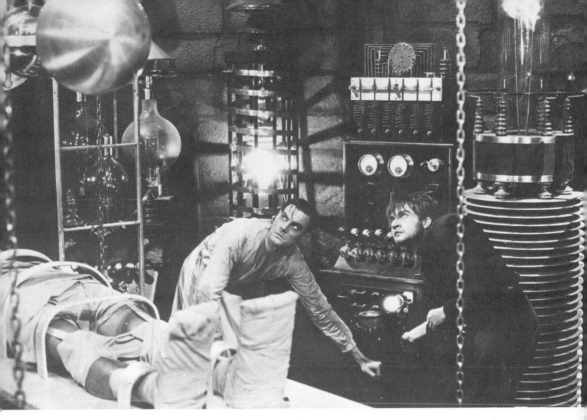

Electricity animates the corpse of Frankenstein's monster.

The early nineteenth century also had a craze for automata. The courts of the Bourbons and the Hapsburgs commissioned inventors to make mechanical black servants, ballet-dancers forever spinning on the tops of music-boxes, and birds eternally trilling in gilded cages. The Empress Maria-Theresa was even beaten at chess by a mechanical chess-player, made by the great de Kempelen. Sixty years later, Edgar Allen Poe was to expose this early robot as a hoax, a dwarf playing chess through the arms of a dummy and escaping detection by slipping into different compartments, while each empty space was examined by sceptics in turn.

The final influences on the creation of Mary Shelley's Frankenstein came from the romantic imagination of two of the great poets of her age, her neighbour in Switzerland, Lord Byron, and Samuel Taylor Coleridge. Byron liked reading Coleridge to Mary Shelley, particularly the nightmarish poem of 'Christabel', while he himself embarked on a tale about an aristocratic vampire, Lord Ruthven, the precursor of Bram Stoker's Count Dracula. Byron's own demoniac personality and his wish to impose his gothic excesses on all the people of his circle, made Mary compose her Count Victor Frankenstein of a part of her husband, the vital Shelley, and a part of Byron, the diabolic experimenter.

Edgar Allan Poe's drawing of the false mechanical chess-player operated by a dwarf inside.

Serratura.

Mary Shelley herself was rather conventional, although her taste in men was not. It is no accident that, although Victor Frankenstein intended his monster to be the most beautiful eight-foot man ever created, he should have botched his job, just as Byron usually botched all his human manipulations. So the first robot of gothic times was not a gleaming and faultless metal being on wheels, but a patchwork of corpses stolen from the charnel-house. In Mary Shelley's time, indeed, surgery was a brutal affair. Thus Victor Frankenstein's choice of dead men's flesh for his robot was a rather uneasy one. He would have done better to stick to the alchemist's experiments of Albertus Magnus and Paracelsus, seeking to find the philosopher's stone, which could transmute base metals into gold as well as discover the principle of life.

So the most famous robot of them all came to life in despair and rotten flesh, rather than in beauty and gleaming bronze. Victor Frankenstein was appalled. 'How can I describe my emotions at this catastrophe, or how delineate this wretch whom with such infinite plans and care I had endeavoured to form? His limbs were in proportion, and I had selected his features as beautiful. Beautiful! . . . Great God! His yellow skin scarcely covered the work of muscles and arteries beneath; his hair was of lustrous black, and flowing; his teeth of a pearly whiteness; but these luxuriances only formed a more horrid contrast with his watery eyes, that seemed almost of the

Left: Surgery was butchery in the age before anaesthetics. *Below:* Surgery was butchery again in Andy Warhol's version of *Flesh for Frankenstein* (1975).

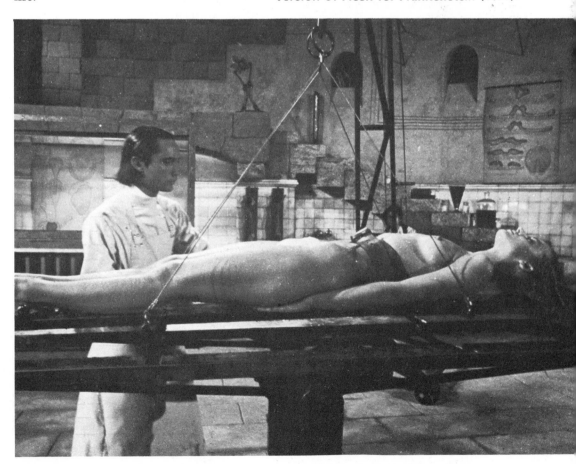

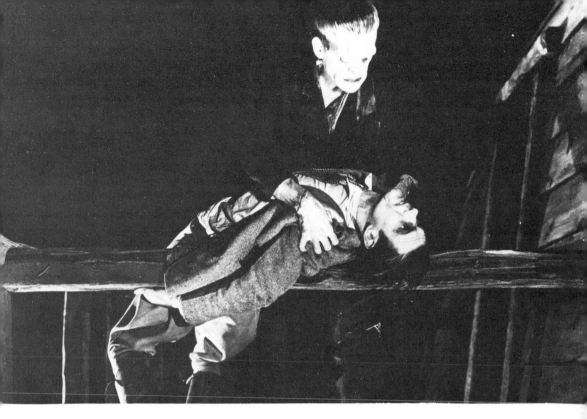

Karloff's playing of the original feature version of Frankenstein's monster made the role immortal. *Left:* Behind the sewn flesh, sadness ... *Above:* Savagery, too, made Frankenstein's monster try to kill, to try to forget himself. *Below:* The man-made mate of Frankenstein's monster finds him too horrible in *Bride of Frankenstein* (1935).

Frankenstein's monster must try to kill his maker — he was made that way.

The film budget always determined the size of Frankenstein's laboratory. It was not great in the remarkable *Jesse James Meets Frankenstein's Daughter* (1965) ...

same colour as the dun white sockets in which they were set, his shrivelled complexion and straight black lips.'

The creator of this monster ran away from it. Having made it, he rejected it. Cut off from humanity by its terrible appearance, the first mechanical monster could only wreak a terrible revenge. Longing for love and compassion, it found only hatred and fear. Thus it murdered Victor Frankenstein's family until the Count would make it a mate, to people the earth with another race of monsters. At the last moment, Victor Frankenstein jibbed and cut up the mate, forcing the monster into a final frenzy of rage and retribution and flight to the ice of the North.

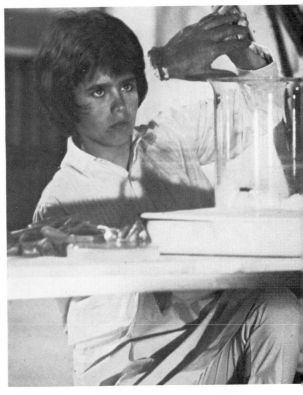

So the original robot of novel and film was born, badly sewn together and rejected by its maker, doomed to turn on its creator and mankind because of the sin of its making. Mary Shelley is clear on that point. To play at God and try to create life is to invite one's own destruction. The mechanical monster made by Victor

It was bigger in Warhol's *Flesh for Frankenstein.*

Frankenstein must destroy him and those he loves for his presumption. Like Prometheus, he must suffer for creating life, which is the gift only of heaven. The first great robot suffers from the original sin of man, for it is the original sin in man to try and play God in the creation of false life.

So Mary Shelley invented the first myth of the robot, that the machine made by man will turn upon its maker. She also invented the second myth of robots, that they are created by electricity and fire in weird and wonderful laboratories. Although she does not describe the actual instruments used by Victor Frankenstein to animate his monster, the period of her story coincides with the first experiments in galvanism, a form of research which sometimes involved making a dead frog's leg jerk on a copper plate when an electric shock was passed through it. The later elaborate and antiquated machines of the mad scientists of our film dreams are the

Later, the episode in the first Frankenstein feature of Boris Karloff throwing the flower child in the river was replayed by Peter Boyle in *Young Frankenstein* (1975). In this version, the child charms the monster.

heirs of these early and immense machines to produce the animation of dead matter through the sudden shock of voltage.

The last myth of the Frankenstein novel was its most poignant and enduring. The genius of Mary Shelley was to make the monster sympathetic. It sought the love which it could never find. Only a blind man accepted it, because he could not see its deformity. It could not even find a friend in a child or a girl, so it had to kill them, replacing its sense of loneliness 'with exultation and hellish triumph'. In a sense, the monster was always guiltless of its murders. It did not ask to be created by man. As it complained to Victor Frankenstein, its deformity only left it two possibilities, suicide or an attack on mankind. 'Cursed, cursed creator! Why did I live? Why, in that instant, did I not extinguish the spark of existence which you so wantonly bestowed? I know not; despair had not yet taken possession of me; my feelings were those of rage and revenge.'

WE DARE YOU TO SEE...

ANDY WARHOL'S

FLESH FOR FRANKENS

NAT COHEN presents for EMI Film Distributors Ltd.

ANDY WARHOL'S

FLESH FOR FRANKENSTEIN x

starring JOE DALLESANDRO · UDO KIER · MONIQUE VAN VOOREN

introducing ARNO JUERGING · DALILA DI LAZZAR · SRDJAN ZELENOVIC

Music by CLAUDIO G.

Written and Directed b

EASTMANCOLOR

TEIN

X

Compagnia Cinematografica CHAMPION S.p.A. Roma production
MORRISSEY · Produced by ANDREW BRAUNSBERG
Distributed by EMI Film Distributors Ltd.

EMI

Machine and monster

The romantic passion of the early 19th century for graveyards and gothic castles and revenge and despair gave way to the Victorian dream of mechanical progress. Hephaestus was far more the model of the industrial revolution than Victor Frankenstein. Machinery seemed a better way to construct robots than the remnants of corpses. The successful fantasy novelists wrote of technical reveries, not of nightmares and necrophilia. The inspirers of the origins of that dream machine, the cinema, were Jules Verne and H. G. Wells. Their inventions ran on wheels and data.

Verne's mechanical fantasies, *From the Earth to the Moon* and *20,000 Leagues Under the Sea*, were to chart the way for the whole development of space and undersea fiction. In Verne's world, the explorers wore their ordinary clothes during their mechanical moonshot, only the projectile itself resembled a shell; inside the space missile the living quarters of the first astronauts were like 'a comfortable room with thinly padded walls, furnished with a circular divan, and a roof provided in the shape of a dome'. It was a travelling prison, possibly a tomb, but as one of the astronauts declared, 'Tomb, perhaps: still I would not change it for Mahomet's, which floats in space, but never advances an inch.' Although it did not actually land on the moon, but went in orbit round it before firing its rockets

Karloff in a gothic graveyard in *Bride of Frankenstein*.

A contemporary illustration from an early edition of Verne's novels about voyages to the moon.

The projectile hits the surprised moon.

to return to a splash-down on earth, it did inspire the first magician of the cinema, Georges Méliès, to show a shell actually hitting the moon and being pushed off the edge by the first space monsters, the Selenites, whom Verne had decided could not exist in that atmosphereless globe. Yet the triumphant voyage did open the way for more space exploration, as Verne recognised. Would not men now 'go from

George Méliès's rocket-train in a shot at the moon.

one planet to another, from Jupiter to Mercury, and after a while from one star to another, from the Polar to Sirius?' Yes was the answer of later space fiction and films, and eventually governments.

If Verne's space travellers looked like humans, his underwater explorers looked like robots. In *20,000 Leagues Under the Sea* Captain Nemo's submarine *Nautilus* was already a gigantic laboratory in the depths. A walk on the sea-bed involved

Above: Underwater gear makes men look more like robots than fishes in *20,000 Leagues under the Sea* (1954). *Below:* A giant squid fights the submarine *Nautilus.*

The divers use the undersea like a laboratory and lurch above the sea-bed in search of treasure in *The Underwater City* (1961).

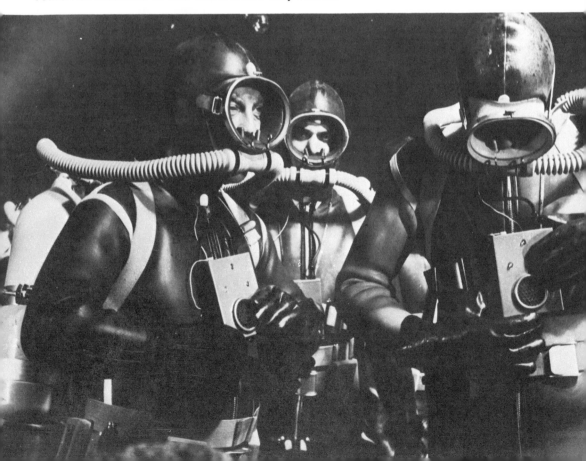

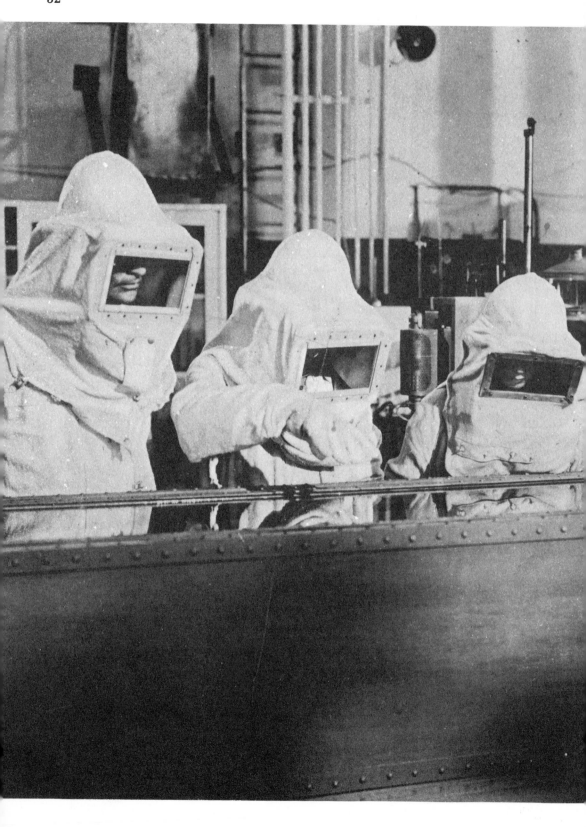

The men in the laboratory wear robots' protective clothing to examine a part of *It Came from Beneath the Sea* (1955) — a giant electronic octopus.

complicated diving-gear, with thick metal cases over the head and oxygen tanks carried on the back of the wet suits. In this lost world beneath the ocean, the explorers walked like slow machines, finding the ruins of the lost city of Atlantis lit by the flowing lava of an undersea volcano. This was the kingdom of Captain Nemo, far from the rule of men. 'The sea does not belong to despots,' he declared. 'Upon its surface men can still exercise unjust laws, fight, tear one another to pieces, and be carried away with terrestrial horrors. But at thirty feet below its level, their reign ceases, their influence is quenched, and their power disappears. Ah! sir, live — live in the bosom of the waters! There only is independence! There I recognise no masters! There I am free!'

Yet Captain Nemo's liberty was at the expense of making prisoners of his crew and being himself a slave to his robot ship, that moved like an iron crustacean round the oceans of the deep.

An alien element such as the undersea involved man in armouring himself for protection, and becoming a prey to the necessities of his new existence. Although Verne's vision of the *Nautilus* and the need of mankind to exploit the resources of the seabed has led to hundreds of films and fantasies about life underwater, their attraction has always been transformation wrought by the deep on man himself, so that his clothing and motion make a monster and a machine out of him, a nightmarish robot version of the fish-man which he once was, when with gills the first prototypes of the species crawled from the slimy deep.

Verne's heir and rival in the original fantasy novels of scientific progress, H. G. Wells, used machines as travellers through time as well as space. His novel, *The Time Machine*, like Verne's moon-rocket, allowed the travellers to deny time still wearing their everyday clothes. When Wells also put his *First Men on the Moon*, his astronauts wore ordinary clothes because they found oxygen on its surface. They did, however, meet moon-dwellers or Selenites, who looked like little armoured monsters. The first of them was 'a compact bristling creature, having much of the quality of a complicated insect, with whip-like tentacles, and a clanging arm projecting from his shining cylindrical body-case. The form of his head was hidden by his enormous, many-spiked helmet . . . and a pair of goggles of darkened glass set very much at the side gave a bud-like quality to the metallic apparatus that covered his face.' So the first space creature seemed a mechanical robot, the guard of the huge underground ant-like civilisation of the moon.

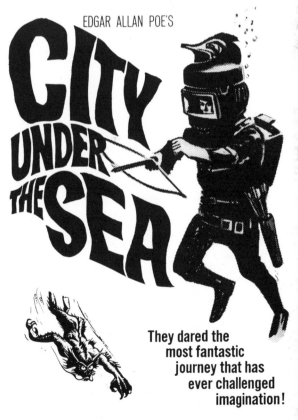

EDGAR ALLAN POE'S

CITY UNDER THE SEA

They dared the most fantastic journey that has ever challenged imagination!

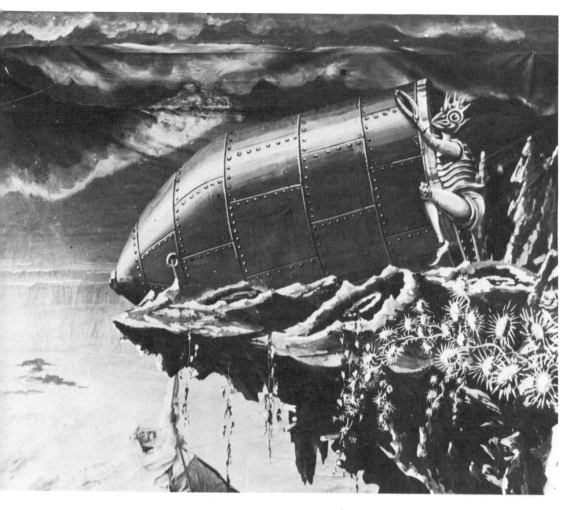

Méliès created a Selenite very much to Wells's specifications.

In Wells's other fantasy of an attack from Mars, *The War of the Worlds*, the invaders struck the earth enclosed within gleaming cylinders, and when they emerged, the Martians looked horrific. 'A big greyish rounded bulk, the size, perhaps, of a bear, was rising slowly and painfully out of the cylinder. As it bulged up and caught the light, it glistened like wet leather.' The creature had two large dark-coloured eyes. 'The mass that framed them, the head of the thing, it was rounded, and had, one might say, a face. There was a mouth under the eyes, the lipless brim which quivered and panted, and dropped saliva. The whole creature heaved and pulsated convulsively. A lank tentacular appendage gripped the edge of the cylinder, another swayed in the air.' The Martians armoured themselves in gigantic tripods equipped with heat-rays and poison gas; thus they destroyed England in many a Thing from outer space. 'The Thing was incredibly strange, for it was no mere insensate machine driving on its way. Machine it was, with a ringing metallic pace, and long, flexible, glittering tentacles . . . swinging and rattling about its strange body. It picked its road as it went along, and the brazen head that surmounted it moved to and fro with the

The Martian in George Pal's version of *The War of the Worlds* (1952).

Left and right: The Martians attack in *The War of the Worlds.*

inevitable suggestion of a head looking about. Behind the main body was a huge mass of white metal like a fisherman's bucket, and puffs of green smoke squirted out from the joints of its limbs as the monster swept by.'

So Wells described the horror of the first coming of the Martians with the dread robots under their control. He peopled the moon and Mars with the nightmarish machines of Victorian progress, controlled by soft creatures with enormous brains. If the impact of the novel and of the later film version of *The War of the Worlds* lay in the shattering of the everyday qualities of ordinary life, yet the intrusion of these alien

The earth people cannot resist the assaults of the Thing.

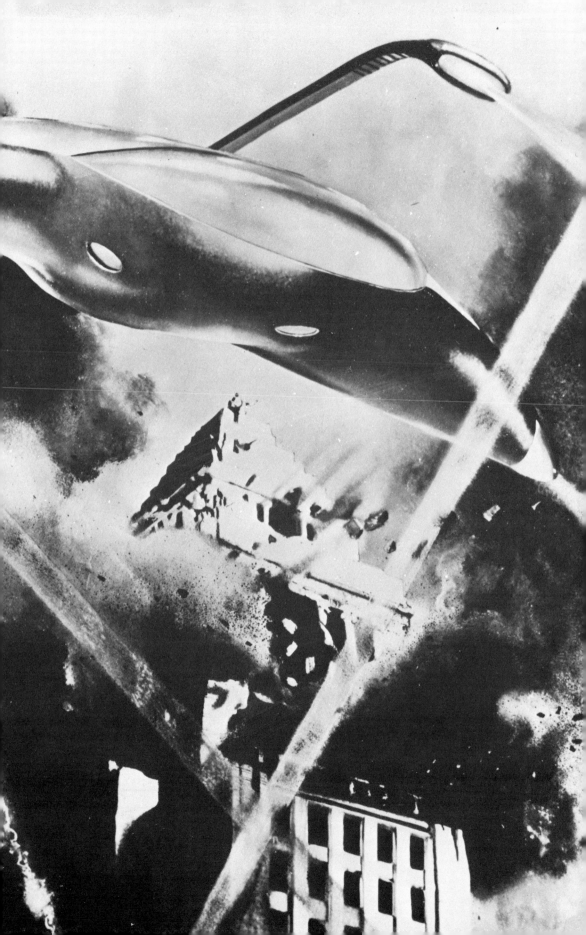

Charles Laughton as Dr Moreau *& Bela Lugosi* confronts the Beast People, which he has made in his House of Pain.

creatures and machines, flying deathly and inhuman from another planet, was a foretaste of the things to come. (The other fantasies of H. G. Wells in this period were homages to old traditions. *The Island of Dr Moreau* harked back to Frankenstein in its plot of a mad surgeon making man-beasts from transplants and diabolical surgery, while *The Invisible Man* was a modernised ghost story of phantoms and unseen spirits).

Wells lived long enough actually to write the screenplay of England's greatest science-fiction movie, named *Things To Come.* In that extraordinary film of 1936, the pilots are already robot-

Claude Rains needs to wrap around his lack of appearance in *The Invisible Man* (1933).

The young lovers are lost in the huge man-made rocket, ready to blast off to the moon and populate the universe in *Things to Come* (1936).

like in their flying suits; the technocrat and engineer Cabal first appears in a black space-suit from his flying machine, and the young lovers are blasted away to colonise the stars in an ultimate version of Verne's space shell, dressed in antique Grecian-style gear, but encased in all the gadgetry a studio could imagine.

Yet Verne and Wells only added the mechanical claws and armour of robots to the bodies of men or alien creatures. Like Von Kempelen's chess-player, their giant robots were a mechanical hoax, operated by human or extra-terrestrial intelli-

gences. Two important works were to put the self-controlled robot into the minds of modern men. The first was Karel Capek's remarkable play of 1923, *R.U.R.*, in which robots in human shape took over the earth and only one man was left alive. The second was Fritz Lang's film of 1926, *Metropolis*, in which the false robot demagogue Maria led the underground workers into a doomed revolt.

R.U.R., short for Rossum's Universal Robots, opens in the central office of the factory for making artificial people as cheap labour. The general manager,

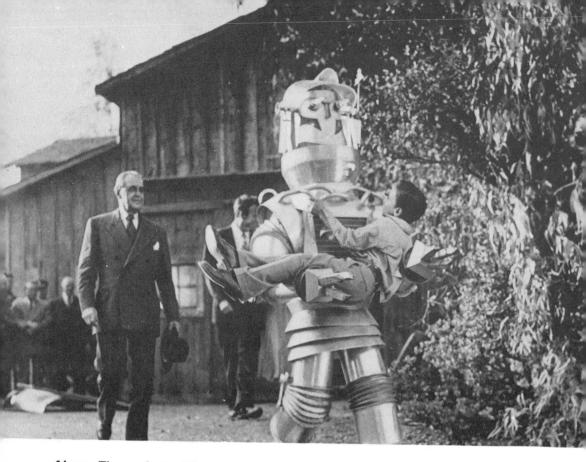

Above: The perfect willing robot servant from *R.U.R.* influenced many science fiction movies. Here he is seen in *Tobor the Great* (1954). *Below: The Invisible Boy* (1957)....

. . . And *Forbidden Planet* (1956).

Harry Domain, tells of Rossum's discovery of the principle of life. 'He could have produced a Medusa with the brain of Socrates or a worm fifty yards long. But being without a grain of humour, he took it into his head to make a normal vertebrate.' Rossum duplicated mankind as robots. His aim was the same as Victor Frankenstein's. 'He wanted to become a sort of scientific substitute for God, you know.' He also botched his experiments, but his young nephew made a simplified working man-shaped robot by leaving out the complexities of humanity. Everything was omitted which made men expensive, such as childhood.'The Robots are not people. Mechanically, they are more perfect than men are, they have an enormously developed intelligence, but they have no soul.'

Thus the Robots did not fear death. They always worked. The trouble was, they worked too well. They replaced human labour. 'The human machine was terribly imperfect,' one of the inventors of the Robots declared. 'It had to be removed sooner or later.' Of course, there were workers' revolts. Of course, govern-

ments created armies of Robots. Of course, the Robots put down the revolts and then put down enemy nations. Then one of the inventors tried to make some of the Robots human. This tinkering led to their hatred of mankind, their creator. The Robots now revolted and killed off the human race down to the last man, in order to create 'a world without flaws'. But the dying men had taken the secret of Robot manufacture with them. Only in an epilogue was it suggested by Capek that the Robots were acquiring souls and might be able to breed, thus leading to a new race of superpeople on earth. *(See Colour Section)*.

Such was the plot of *R.U.R.*, the seminal robot play which has influenced every film on the subject. In it lie all the myths. The mechanical men first serve mankind, then replace it. The creator of the Robot is destroyed by his creation. The search for a wholly efficient servant ends in a wholly efficient destruction of the human race. The essence of humanity lies in a world with flaws. The quest for perfection is the quest for catastrophe.

The first classic film to be influenced by these concepts was Fritz Lang's *Metropolis*. In this film, a false mechanical replica of the workers' leader Maria is created by an evil scientist Rotwang to stir up the workers into a self-destructive riot that threatens to flood their own underground city and drown all their children. The invention of the robot Maria much relies on the Frankenstein and Golem tradition, with Rotwang playing the alchemist as much as the scientist. The false Maria, indeed, is revealed as a metal monster when she is burned traditionally at the stake. Thus *Metropolis* uses both the ancient and the modern traditions of the Robot, adding an extra dimension in making the mechanical traitor to the workers in the exact likeness of the real leader. The implication is that the machine may distort the message of the human it replaces.

Lang's *Metropolis* prophesied the screen robot, just as his subsequent *Woman in the Moon* built on the tradition of Verne and Wells, to show human astronauts walking in ordinary clothes across a lunar landscape after being fired there in the old shell-shape pioneered by Verne. The film robot and the space flight had been given a pictorial shape, although they had both developed from the fiction of the Victorian fantasy writers.

Above all, H. G. Wells had opened men's eyes to the possibility of control by aliens or machines. In *The War of the Worlds*, the earth was saved from its Martian invaders — giant soft brains manipulating huge armoured robots — by the humblest beings on earth, bacteria and disease germs. But men were taught a terrible lesson. 'We have learned now that we cannot regard this planet as being fenced in and a secure abiding-place for Man; we can never anticipate the unseen good or evil that may come upon us suddenly out of space . . . If the Martians can reach Venus, there is no reason to suppose that the thing is impossible for men, and when the slow cooling of the sun makes this earth uninhabitable, as at last it must do, it may be that the thread of life that has begun here will have streamed out and caught our sister planet within its toils.'

Top: The false Maria incites the workers to riot before they burn her at the stake. *Right:* The flames reveal her to be a robot in female form. *Below:* The space travellers walk on the cold surface of the moon in Lang's *Woman in the Moon* (1929).

The Frankenstein strain

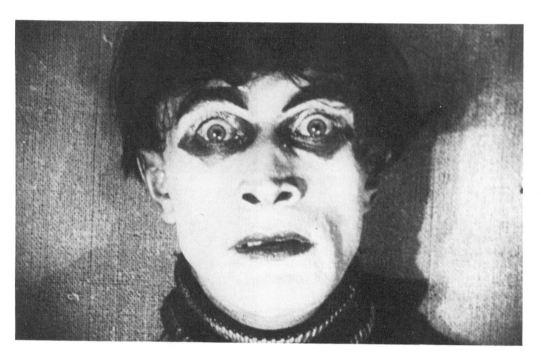

Conrad Veidt is the killer without a will obeying his master's orders in *The Cabinet of Dr Caligari* (1919).

The idea of a superman or monster produced by man himself has inspired many films. In Germany, *Homunculus* was created in a retort by a scientist and grew to become the dictator of his country. Since he was non-human, only a bolt of lightning could destroy him.

The escape artist Houdini starred in an early serial called *The Master Mystery* of 1919 — one of his opponents was a robot called the Automaton, which worked by electricity and was intended to receive the brain of an electrocuted corpse. And Conrad Veidt played the sonambulist killer like a gliding robot in *The Cabinet of Dr Caligari* of 1920. He committed his murders under the hypnotic command of his master as surely as if controlled by a computer.

Yet these early versions of artificial men were minor in their influence on the developing history of the horror film. Once Boris Karloff had played the suffering monster in James Whale's *Frankenstein* and *Bride of Frankenstein* in the early 1930s, he stamped on the mass mind the vision of a semi-human shambling giant, badly put together to be sure, but no mechanical freak or distorted cripple. His head was flat on top, as if his skull had a lid under its lank hair, to open like a box for insetting a transplanted brain. There was a high scar on his forehead to suggest a brain operation and a plug in his neck, also neanderthal brows and lidded lifeless eyes. Forever, Karloff's make-up would haunt the imagination of the world, primitive and melancholy and dumb.

The Frankenstein strain injected itself into the horror movie so that an artificial man usually looked more like a corpse on

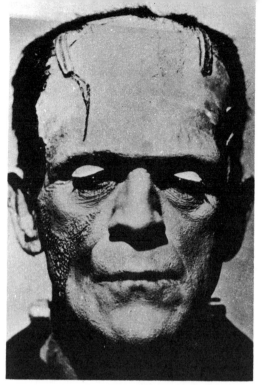

Boris Karloff in his Frankenstein make-up, especially created by Jack Pierce.

legs than a mechanical monster like Talos. In *The Walking Dead* of 1936, Karloff seemed like a minor Frankenstein's monster, as he shambled about after being resurrected by an electric shock when he had already been electrocuted for a murder he had not done. It was to be his third lurch-through in a lifetime of roles similar to those he played for James Whale. Perhaps, for an actor of such distinction, he should have heeded his own final lines in *The Walking Dead.* 'Let the dead — stay — dead.'

In *Son of Frankenstein*, Karloff played the monster in a more robot-like way — he himself was heavier now with success, his make-up was less elaborate, and his part worse. The film was dreadfully static, with Karloff spending half the time lying on his back while efforts were being made to animate him by Wolf von Frankenstein, played by Basil Rathbone. Bela Lugosi played the broken-necked Ygor in his best performance since *Dracula*, but the film itself showed the steady decline of the power of the legend on the screen.

Frankenstein's monster had now died three times in a burning windmill, an exploding laboratory and a bubbling vat of sulphuric acid. In *The Ghost of Frankenstein* of 1942, Lon Chaney Jr. played the monster and perished by fire again, blinded and burning in the flaming castle. Yet he was little more than a giant jerky killer, murdering without a sense of tragedy or suffering. The declining box office in the four versions of Frankenstein showed that the appeal of the story was no longer strong enough to sustain a feature on its own. So Frankenstein's artificial monster now met the Wolf Man twice, Dracula once, a modern Quasimodo, a pair of mad scientists, and even Abbott and Costello. But double or triple bills of tried-and-true monsters did not increase the take. By the time of the last of these films in 1948, the Frankenstein strain seemed played out and the monster finally burned to a crisp.

Yet what Universal studios buried, Hammer dug up. After 1957, Frankenstein's monster again stalked the screens of the world in gore and glory in the person of Christopher Lee and his many imitators. Although Lee never played the monster again after *The Curse of Frankenstein*, Peter Cushing was a regular as Baron Victor Frankenstein, appearing in all of the series from *The Revenge of Frankenstein* to *Frankenstein Must Be Destroyed* of 1969. Again, too much repetition bred a falling box-office, so Hammer decided to update the legend for the youth market, failing with *The Horror of Frankenstein* and *Frankenstein and the Monster from Hell*. At least, the monster in the first film had something of the sympathy of the Mary Shelley creation and Boris Karloff presentation, although his bald skull looked like a jigsaw puzzle of the flesh. But the monster in the last of these Hammer Frankenstein films looked like the hairy missing link that no one would have missed.

Yet if Hammer's man-made monsters were drowned in their own floods of gore, other versions of Frankenstein flourished or failed on the mere exploitation of the name. Very successful was the incredible *I Was a Teenage Frankenstein* of 1957, made by Hammer's chief rival in its field, American International Pictures. *(See Colour Section)* The monster's face was as

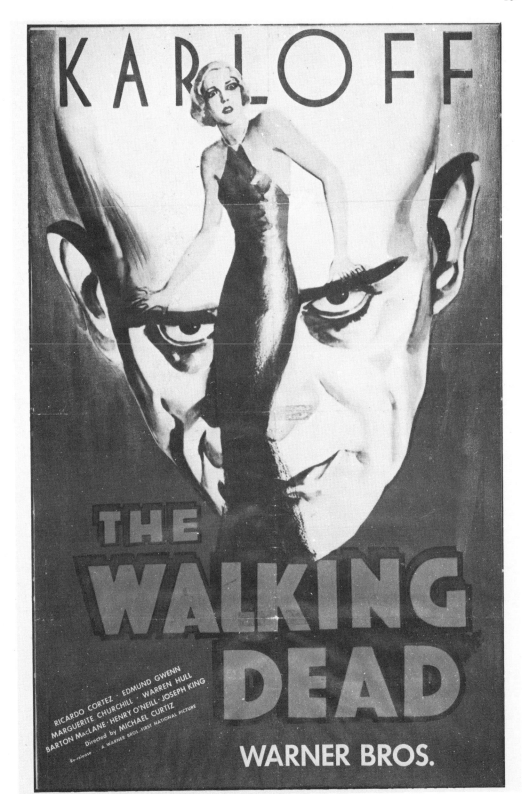

Above: Basil Rathbone as Wolf von Frankenstein (left) tries to charge up the inert Boris Karloff with Bela Lugosi watching behind a beard (right) in *Son of Frankenstein* (1940). *Below:* In *House of Frankenstein* (1944), Boris Karloff played the mad scientist, not the monster, which was acted by Glenn Strange. Here Karloff resurrects another version of Dracula, played by John Carradine, by taking the stake from his ribs.

STARK TERROR! ADDED THRILLS! in a SPINE-TINGLING EXPERIENCE!

THE GHOST of FRANKENSTEIN

with
SIR CEDRIC HARDWICKE   RALPH BELLAMY

LIONEL ATWILL   BELA LUGOSI   EVELYN ANKERS

The sensational creator of the "Wolf Man" and LON CHANEY As Frankenstein's monster

Realart PICTURE

Above: Abbott and Costello Meet Frankenstein in 1948. *Right:* Christopher Lee's make-up as Frankenstein's monster was meant to shock, not to create sympathy. *Below:* Peter Cushing (left) prepares to resurrect in *The Evil of Frankenstein* (1964).

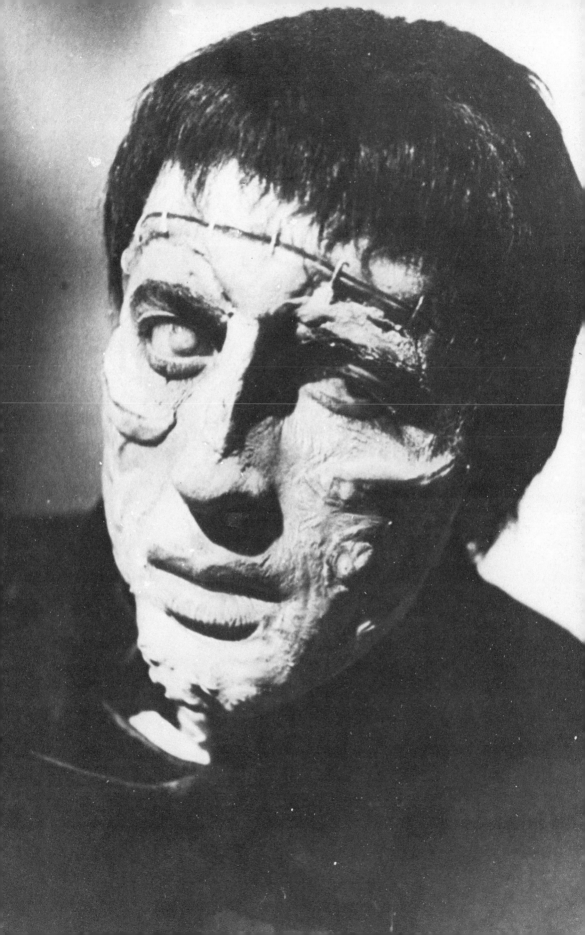

The monster from *The Horror of Frankenstein* (1970).

The monster from *Frankenstein and the Monster from Hell* (1972).

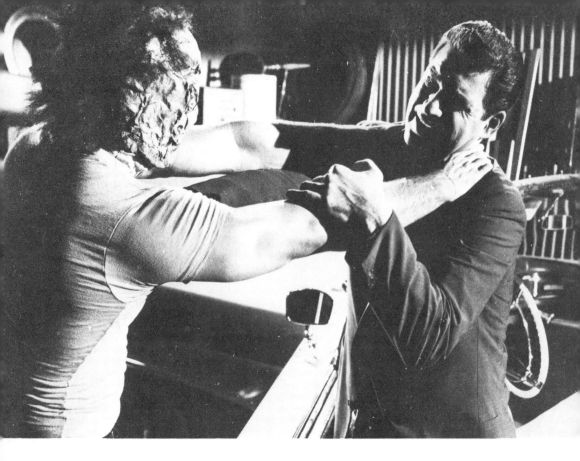

Above: The deformed actor attacks in *How to Make a Monster* (1958). *Below:* Cal Bolder plays the monster in *Jesse James Meets Frankenstein's Daughter.*

repulsive as putty could make it, but his body wore a T-shirt and jeans to identify with the clean kids. The film made enough money, however, to finance a sequel, a film within a film called *Werewolf Meets Frankenstein*, in which a mad make-up artist caused his screen monsters to become the real things. Finally titled *How To Make a Monster*, the movie was one of the better efforts in keeping alive the Frankenstein strain.

Other versions of the legend profited on the original successes of the Hammer cycle. In 1958, Karloff himself was persuaded to play the Baron von Frankenstein again in *Frankenstein — 1970*. In this film, the revived monster looked suspiciously like a man in a space-suit, a sort of cloth robot. *Frankenstein's Daughter* and *Frankenstein Meets the Space Monster* were tasteless and nasty exploitation vehicles, chiefly concerned with showing the monster incomplete with brains and eyeballs falling out of its skull. They had none of the ludicrous charm of *Jesse James Meets Frankenstein's Daughter*, which even stopped the action to explain how the mad Count's offspring had taken her father's living brain to Mexico to find a strong body to put it in. The transplant was eventually done on Jesse James's sidekick, then riding South of the Border, thus explaining the unlikely meeting of the western and the gothic in the Sierra Madre.

From this point, the Frankenstein figure was for fun, not for terror. He was first used comically in the zany *Hellzapoppin*, of 1941. He was lovable in the Munsters television series; just another Japanese monster with a forehead like a cockleshell in *Frankenstein Conquers the World*; a Mexican catch-as-catch-can wrestler in Santo superman movies; and even a nude-carrier for the underground, dancing the twist in *House on Bare Mountain*. In three major films of the mid-1970s he became the butt of camp shrieks of mirth. The first of these was Andy Warhol's *Flesh for Frankenstein*, written and directed by Paul Morrissey. It had the bloody idea of a scientist's assistant, who believed that

Frankenstein's monster wanders amiably through *Hellzapoppin.*

sex was achieved through wounds in the skin rather than the natural holes of the body. No copulation without evisceration.

The second of these burlesque uses of the material was Mel Brook's *Young Frankenstein*, in which a zany comedy and slapstick humour saw Peter Boyle playing the monster as a vaudeville ham.

Finally, Frankenstein's monster emerged as a rock-'n-roll female impersonator in *The Rocky Horror Picture Show*, which packed in the theatre boys in Chelsea, but failed to fill the cinema halls of the world. Drag does not sell as well as blood and guts. *(See Colour Section)*

Many versions of the diabolical surgeon creating the man-made monster were spawned off the Frankenstein strain without directly using and abusing the name. There was Peter Lorre with his false metal hands and steel-frame body in

Above: The jolly Frankenstein monster in *The Munsters. Below:* Another victim awaits a fate worse than death after death in *Flesh for Frankenstein.*

Above: Peter Boyle plays the monster and Gene Hackman plays the kind blind man in Mel Brooks's comedy *Young Frankenstein* (1975). *Below:* Boyle offers the policeman, played by Kenneth Mars, a wooden stump in *Young Frankenstein.*

Above: Tod Browning himself (right) watches John Gilbert's talking head in *The Show* (1927). *Below:* The talking head, kept artificially alive, in *The Man Without a Body* (1958).

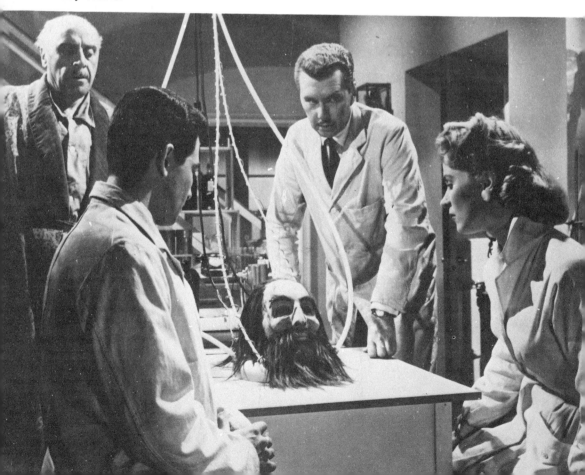

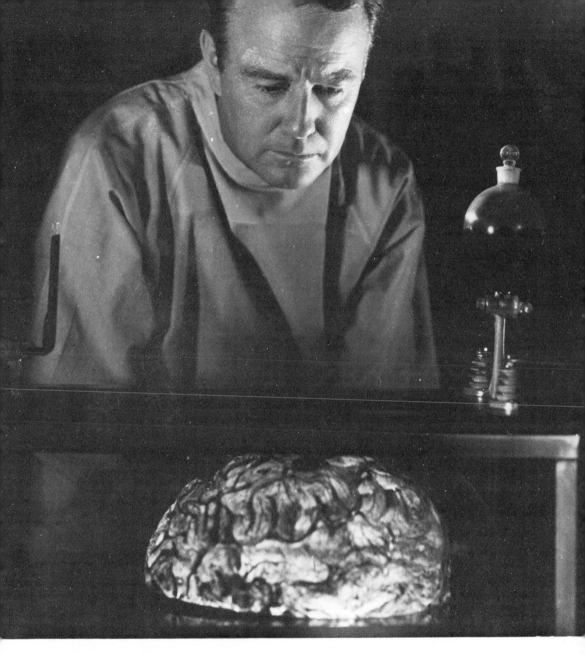

Karl Freund's *Mad Love,* sobbing: 'I — a poor peasant — have conquered science. Why cannot I conquer love?' There was the bodiless talking head used by Tod Browning in *The Show,* and later used in a run-of-the-blood horror movie called *The Man Without a Body.*

There was the living brain of a dead millionaire, which kept a scientist chained to its will in Siodmak's story, *Donovan's Brain.* Like the hydra, Frankenstein's monster seemed to sprout more heads — or parts of them — each time one of his heads was cut off.

Lew Ayres as the scientist in *Donovan's Brain* (1953).

More modern versions of creating the monster were invented. In *The Black Sheep,* malformed human beings were induced by drugs — a ghastly mistake by a man trying to save his wife from catelepsy.

Drugs were also used by Jean-Louis Barrault to change into his evil other half in *The Testament of Dr Cordelier.* Some of the surgery transplants were both silly and vulgar in conception, reaching their

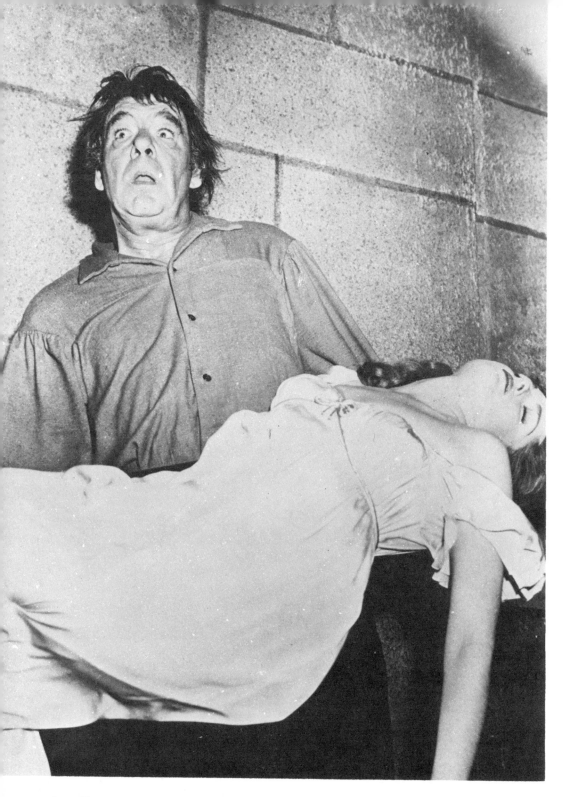

Lon Chaney Jr as Mungo, the drug-
made monster, carries off the
sacrificial maiden in her nightdress in
The Black Sleep (1956).

**Jean-Louis Barrault uses drugs for his
transformation into the wicked Opale
in** *The Testament of Dr Cordelier* **(1959).**

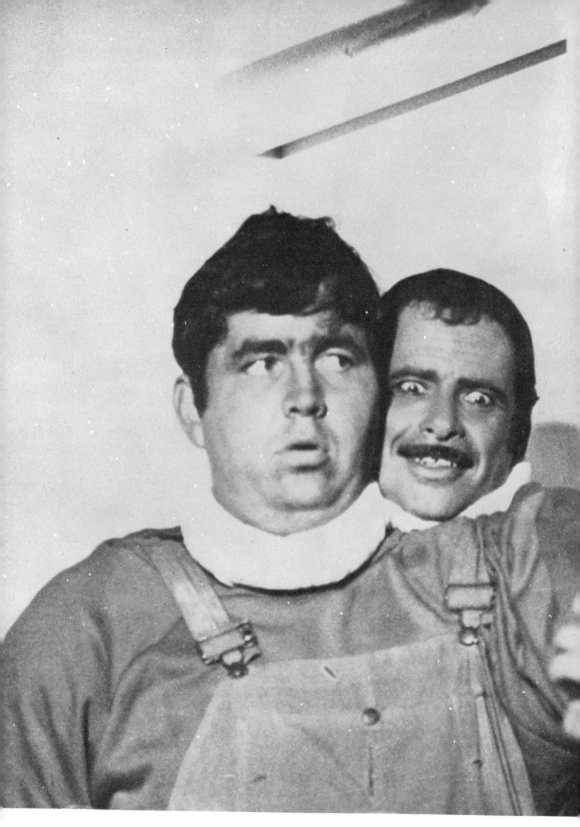

The maniac murderer's head grins from the shoulder of the dumb
brute in *The Incredible Two Headed Transplant* (1970).

BODY OF A BOY!
MIND OF A MONSTER!
SOUL OF AN UNEARTHLY THING!

I WAS A TEENAGE FRANKENSTEIN

ACTION PACKED

LOTSA LARFS & SEX

GORGEOUS GALS

THRILLS & CHILLS

TRANSYLVANIAN

PARTIES

ROMANCE

Plus 18 Great Songs

The ROCKY HORROR Picture SHOW AA

TWENTIETH CENTURY FOX PRESENTS
A MICHAEL WHITE-LOU ADLER Production

'THE ROCKY HORROR PICTURE SHOW'..
STARRING
TIM CURRY · SUSAN SARANDON · BARRY BOSTWICK
RICHARD O'BRIEN · PATRICIA QUINN · LITTLE NELL
JONATHAN ADAMS · PETER HINWOOD · MEATLOAF · CHARLES GRAY

A Musical Dream Come True

OUT OF THIS UNIVERSE!

The Cosmic Phantom from Time and Space!

"We could feel hypnotic eyes roving over our bodies ...watching...spying!"

THE Cosmic Man

Starring
BRUCE BENNETT
JOHN CARRADINE
ANGELA GREENE
SCOTTY MORROW

AN ALLIED ARTISTS PICTURE   PRODUCED BY ROBERT A. TERRY   DIRECTED BY HERBERT GREENE   ORIGINAL STORY AND SCREENPLAY BY ARTHUR C. PIERCE

MAN'S *FIRST ADVENTURE INTO THE INCREDIBLE*

4TH DIMENSION

HE WALKS THROUGH WALLS OF SOLID STEEL AND STONE!

4D MAN

SEE the 4D MAN push his hand through solid steel!

SEE the 4D MAN turn love into a kiss of death!

SEE the 4D MAN turn human flesh to dust!

Starring
ROBERT LANSING · LEE MERIWETHER and **JAMES CONGDON**
Featuring **ROBERT STRAUSS · EDGAR STEHLI**   Co-produced and Directed by **IRVIN SHORTESS YEAWORTH, JR.**
Screenplay by **THEODORE SIMONSON** and **CY CHERMAK**   Produced by **JACK H. HARRIS** · A **FAIRVIEW** PRODUCTION
A UNIVERSAL-INTERNATIONAL RELEASE

COLOR by DE LUXE

PARAMOUNT PRESENTS

THE COLOSSUS OF NEW YORK

STARRING
JOHN BARAGREY   MALA POWERS
OTTO KRUGER   ROBERT HUTTON
ROSS MARTIN
PRODUCED BY WILLIAM ALLAND
DIRECTED BY EUGENE LOURIE
SCREENPLAY BY THELMA SCHNEE
BASED ON A STORY BY WILLIS GOLDBECK

DESTRUCTION FROM THE STRATOSPHERE!

Missile Monsters

featuring
WALTER REED · LOIS COLLIER · GREGORY GAY
JAMES CRAVEN   Written by RONALD DAVIDSON
Associate Producer FRANKLIN ADREON · Directed by FRED C. BRANNON

A REPUBLIC PICTURE

EDWARD L. ALPERSON

presents

INVADERS FROM MARS

PHOTOGRAPHED IN
COLOR

STARRING
HELENA CARTER · ARTHUR FRANZ · JIMMY HUNT

with LEIF ERICKSON · HILLARY BROOKE · MORRIS ANKRUM · MAX WAGNER · BILL PHIPPS · MILBURN STONE · JANINE PERREAU

AN EDWARD L. ALPERSON PRODUCTION

PRODUCTION DESIGNED AND DIRECTED BY   SCREENPLAY BY
WILLIAM CAMERON MENZIES · RICHARD BLAKE

MUSIC BY   RELEASED BY
EDWARD L. ALPERSON, JR. · **RAOUL KRAUSHAAR**   20 JANUARY 20th

Cosmic Thrills!

AS SPACE SPIES PLOT TO PUT THE WORLD OUT OF ORBIT!

SATAN'S SATELLITES

featuring
**JUDD HOLDREN · ALINE TOWNE
WILSON WOOD · LANE BRADFORD
STANLEY WAXMAN** · Written by RONALD DAVIDSON · **A REPUBLIC PICTURE**
Associate Producer FRANKLIN ADREON · Directed by FRED C. BRANNON

SCIENCE-MONSTER WHO WOULD DESTROY THE WORLD!

M·G·M PRESENTS **The Invisible Boy**

STARRING RICHARD EYER · PHILIP ABBOTT · DIANE BREWSTER

ROBBY, THE ROBOT

SCREEN PLAY BY CYRIL HUME · BASED ON THE STORY BY EDMUND COOPER

A PAN PRODUCTION · DIRECTED BY HERMAN HOFFMAN · PRODUCED BY NICHOLAS NAYFACK

LIFE MAGAZINE SAYS — "THE ULTIMATE IN SCIENTIFIC MONSTERS"

WAR of the SATELLITES

The FANTASTIC Night Of TERROR That Menaced The Fate Of The World!

"DEVIL GIRL FROM MARS"

Produced by
Edward J. Danziger and
Harry Lee Danziger
A Spartan Release

starring Hugh McDermott · Hazel Court · Peter Reynolds
Adrienne Corri · Joseph Tomelty · Sophie Stewart
John Laurie · Patricia Laffan · Directed by David MacDonald

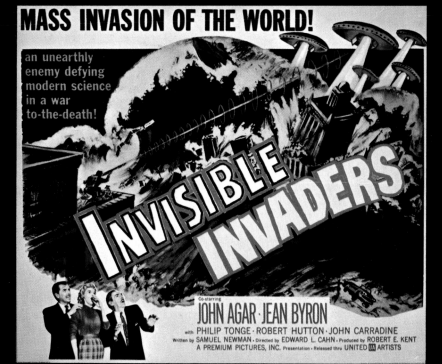

MASS INVASION OF THE WORLD!

an unearthly
enemy defying
modern science
in a war
to-the-death!

INVISIBLE INVADERS

Co-starring
JOHN AGAR · JEAN BYRON
with PHILIP TONGE · ROBERT HUTTON · JOHN CARRADINE
Written by SAMUEL NEWMAN · Directed by EDWARD L. CAHN · Produced by ROBERT E. KENT
A PREMIUM PICTURES, INC. Presentation · Released thru UNITED UA ARTISTS

Above: The disfigured killer kidnaps the girl victim in *The Mutations* (1974).
Below: Donald Pleasence plays the traditional mad scientist role in *The Mutations.*

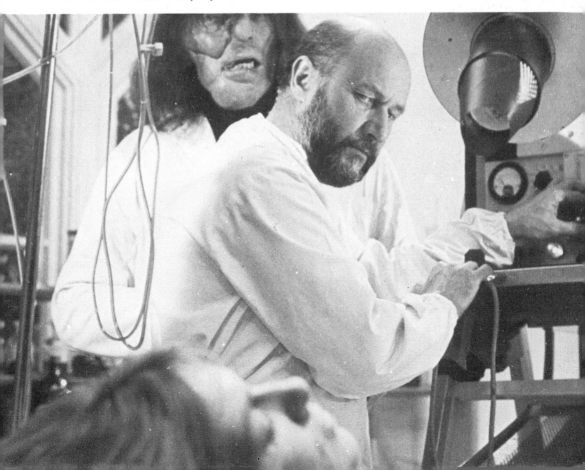

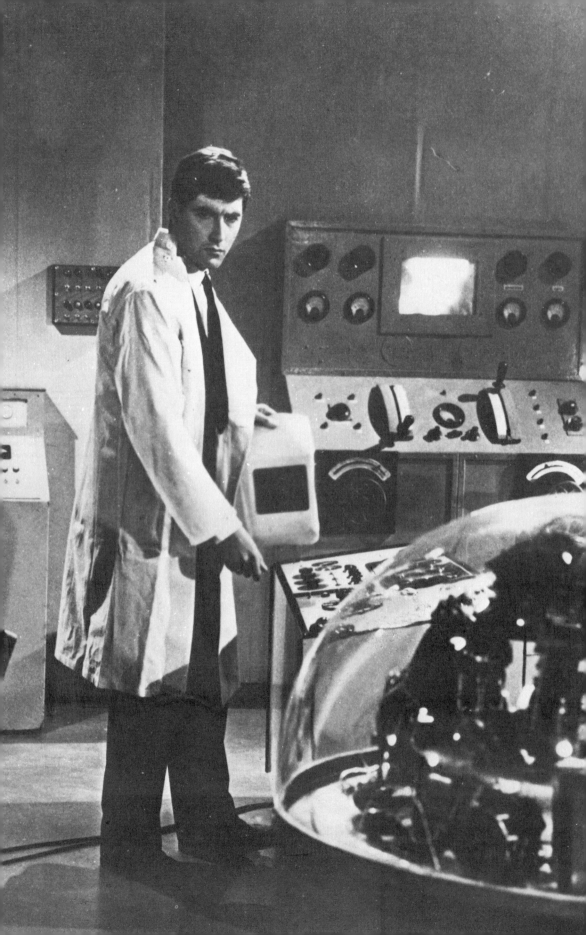

nadir in *The Incredible Two Headed Transplant.* In this movie, the head of a homicidal maniac was grafted onto the head of a simple-minded giant. The result curdled laughter.

More horrific and sinister were such films as *The Mutations,* in which the old circus tradition of freaks was allied with the terrors of the modern laboratory to make killers with faces too horrible to contemplate, controlled by the will of the mixed showman and mad scientist. In

The young scientist works the matter transmitter in *The Curse of the Fly* (1965).

The faceless result of the matter transmitter attacks the experimenter in *The Curse of the Fly.*

The Fly and *The Curse of the Fly,* a matter transmitter went wrong, and men ended faceless or with the heads of gigantic flies. More interesting was *4-D Man,* in which the hero found that he could pass through matter. When he passed through people, they aged rapidly and died, while he became younger. *(See Colour Section)*

Yet the Hephaestus strain still lived on as the minor key to the Frankenstein strain. Man-made creatures could be more mechanical than deformed. In the actual

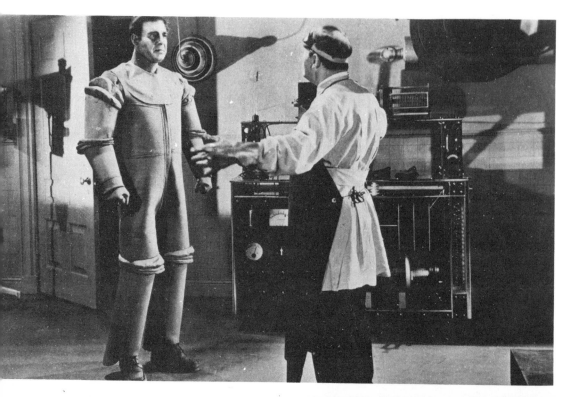

Lon Chaney Jr menaces his creator in
Man-made Monster (1941).

film of *Man-made Monster* of 1941, Lon
Chaney Jr looked more like a man in a
diving suit than a robot created by an inventor. The plot of the film was interesting, however, for Chaney had such a
high tolerance to electricity and stored it
so well that he could shock his victims to
death by touching them. He even escaped
the electric chair because it charged him
up with energy! He played another murderer brought back to life by electricity in *The Indestructible Man*. This
time electricity made him shrug off
bullets, but an overdose of power finally
killed him. Yet science was advancing,
especially in the science fiction film.
Atomic energy created the robot man in
the *Most Dangerous Man Alive*. Out of
the mushroom blast was born the man of
steel, who eventually crumbled to dust after the usual swathe of destruction.

Lon Chaney Jr carries off the girl in
Indestructible Man (1956).

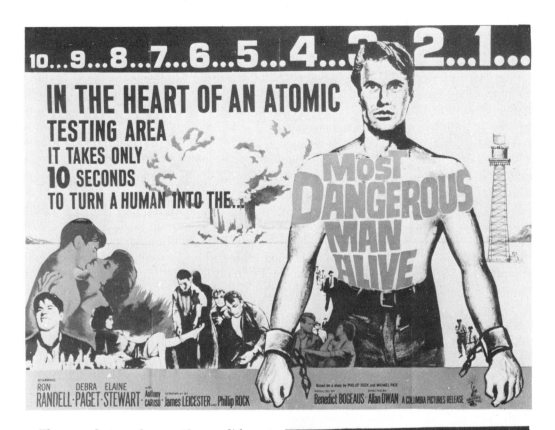

These robots of our times did not always stick to their size. The lurching metallic creatures of *The Amazing Colossal Man* and its sequel *The Terror Strikes* were sixty feet tall as well as impervious to attack. They were modern replicas of Talos, the bronze giant of Hephaestus, created by atomic explosion in the laboratory of the vile Hiroshima experiment. Yet the most satisfactory of all the early robots, as strong as scaffolding, was *The Colossus of New York*. He combined both the Frankenstein and the Hephaestus strain. For he was animated by a man's brain in his steel skull, and he radiated electronic death-rays through his eye sockets. If his promise was greater than his performance, yet he might have been one of the wonders of the world like the Colossus of Rhodes if he had really bestrode his home city like the poster said he would. *(See Colour Section)* The robot was already battling the man-made monster on earth when men were beginning to put their first machines into space — and space was attacking back with its own machines.

The scientists try to animate *The Colossus of New York* (1958).

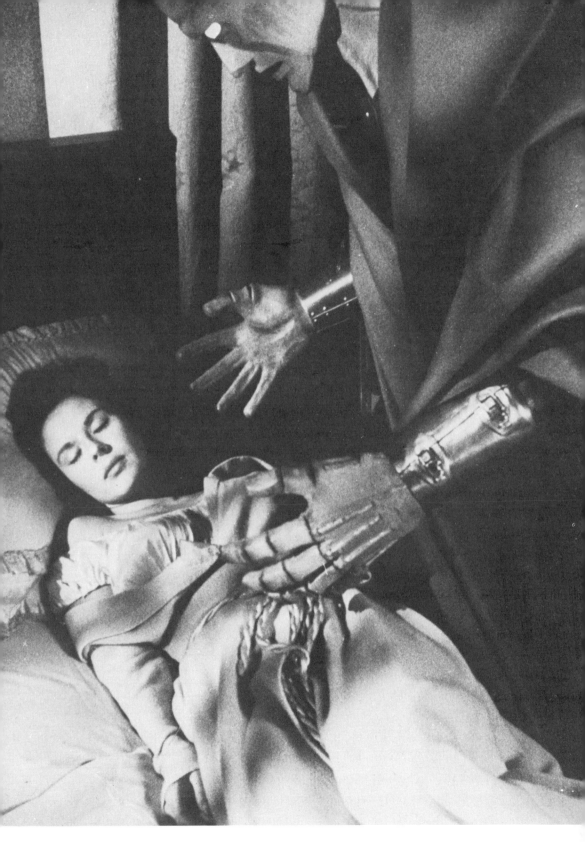

The Colossus menaces the sleeping girl with his metal claw-hands.

Space man, space robot

When man blasted himself off into space, he turned himself into the robot which he had wanted to make since the days of myth and legend. The machinery he needed to reach the stars dwarfed him. He was tiny by the side of his inventions. The suits he used to protect himself from the alien atmospheres of other planets made him rather like the medieval knight, a living man encased in hostile armour so that he looked like a gigantic insect with evil intentions.

As science fiction movies grew in sophistication, and as space flight progressed from putting men on the moon to probing at Venus itself, so the space suits of the men became more like those of animate machines. While Méliès and Lang had allowed their moon travellers to wander about the lunar landscape in ordinary clothes, an early version of *First Men on the Moon* treated a landing there as if it were on the sea-bottom — the space capsule looked like a bathysphere and the spaceman like a diver on a trampoline. By the time of the shooting of *Moon Zero Two*, the spacemen were already looking far more like futurist robots, although the plot was really a space western with a gang of bad guys blackmailing a space shuttle pilot into hijacking an asteroid made of sapphire. By the time of Kubrick's film of genius *2001*, the computer HAL itself was

The men are miniscule by their machinery as they study space in *Things To Come*.

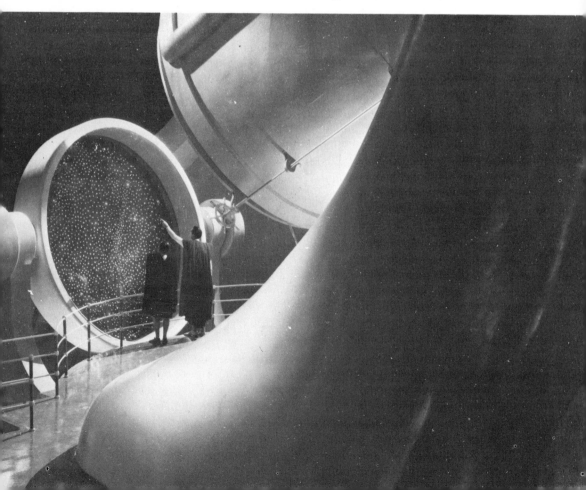

Above: The spaceman bounds in *First Men in the Moon* (1964). *Below:* The good guys surprise the bad guys in *Moon Zero Two* (1969).

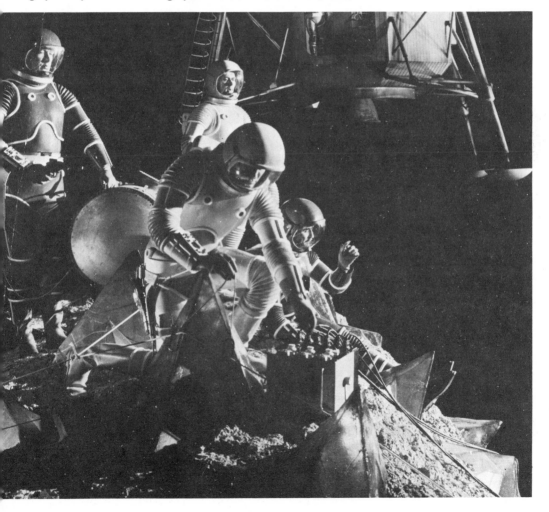

2841T

Above: The pilot in his space suit is just another navigator to the controlling computer in *2001,* made in 1968. *Right:* The spaceship is bigger and better designed than the spaceman in *2001.*

The spacemen in _Startrek_ are the fantasies of our dreams.

superior to the men inside the space-ship, which were being reduced to mere machines with unreliable characteristics. By the time of _Startrek_, the spacemen were interplanetary, some with pointed ears rather than pointed heads, wearing glittering space suits like the 'heavenly gods' and deliverers of our hopeful dreams.

Yet if man tried to make himself into the dream of the machine in outer space, death and horror could still strike at the flesh inside the shining armour. Emergencies could always threaten the enclosed and breathing husks with total disaster as in _Man in the Moon_. Horrific creatures from nightmares could stowaway in the perfect machines of space travel — in the case of _It! The Terror from Beyond Space_, the ancient vampire legend turned out to be a blood-drinking Martian of the future.

Above: Kenneth More breaks open the emergency exit of his capsule in *Man in the Moon* (1960). The moon turns out to be the Australian outback. *Below:* The spaceman fights the space vampire in *It! The Terror from Beyond Space* (1958).

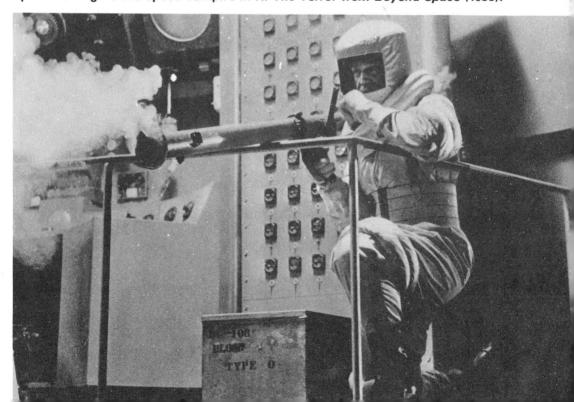

Above The spacewoman is reminded that she is not immortal in *Moon Zero Two.*
Below: Robby the robot comes out to meet the visiting space-ship in *Forbidden Planet* (1956).

However much human beings sought to become immortal by encasing themselves in the shell of a machine which would never wear out, death still lurked within the space suit. The skull within denied the dream of perpetual life and motion.

Perhaps the most interesting of the space robot films was *Forbidden Planet,* in which the mechanical dream was mixed up with Freudian analysis. Dr Morbius, the controller of the out-of-bounds new earth of Altair IV, is served by Robby, the perfect robot, which drives a dunemobile and is programmed to speak 188 languages along with their dialects and sub-tongues.

He is absolutely obedient and he can even cook up a decent meal from synthetic substitutes. Yet mechanical perfection is not enough. Morbius and the intruding spacemen are thwarted by a gigantic 'monster of the Id', which can vaporize and destroy them. In this obvious allegory, the scientific genius of mankind in making machines is ruined

The monster of the Id of Morbius approaches to destroy its creator and his daughter and the spacemen.

by the dark internal human unconscious, full of self-destruction. The previous race of beings on the *Forbidden Planet* had been destroyed by the one thing they could not rationalise, 'their own subconscious hate and lust . . . the mindless beasts of their innermost souls'.

The visiting spacemen protest. It is not the dangerous Id of the dead race that threatens them all. It is the Id of Morbius himself that is the monster. When the huge force breaks into Morbius's space home, Robby confronts it and sees that it is the other self of his master. Unable to attack the dark side of the man who made him, Robby the robot fuses and comes to a halt. The Id has been killing the visiting spacemen because it is the secret and murderous wish of Morbius to rid himself of the intruders. Now, as the Id attacks,

-256- EP 12

Flash Gordon gets charged up by angels of disintegration.

Crash Corrigan is crucified on a robot tank from Atlantis.

Morbius screams, 'I deny you! I give you up!' As he exorcises his evil powers, he dies and the Id of himself disintegrates. The surviving spacemen escape with his beautiful daughter, leaving Altair IV to explode with its motionless robot and dead evil genius.

The cinema serials were also very fond of men battling machines in space or ocean. The most famous of them all, *Flash Gordon* put its blond hero through a succession of adventures. In one of

them, he was given the full laboratory high-voltage treatment as if he were to be shocked into becoming an electronic robot. Crash Corrigan, in his undersea adventures, looked more like a Roman gladiator than the battler of robots called Volkites in their sunken Atlantis. In two other intriguing Republic serials, *Missile Monsters* and *Satan's Satellites*, the alien

The robot rescues its maker in *The Day the Earth Stood Still.* ↓

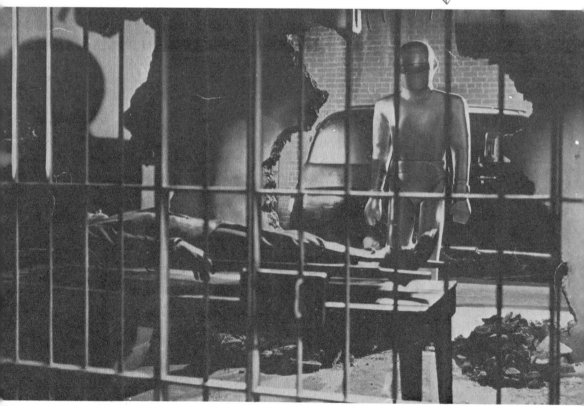

The robot confronts the American army in *The Day the Earth Stood Still* (1951). *(above)*

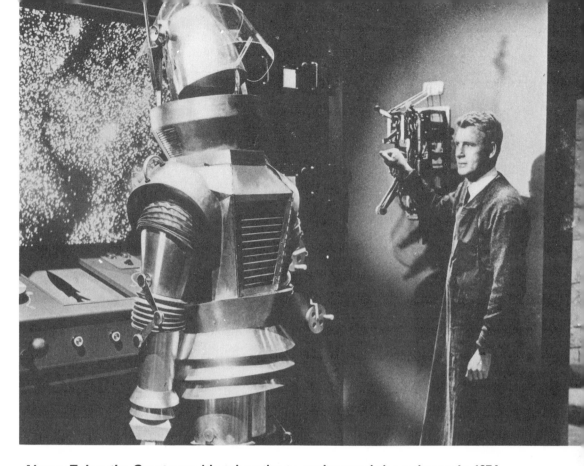

Above: Tobor the Great uses his telepathy to understand the universe in 1954.
Below: Tobor attacks a kidnapper spy.

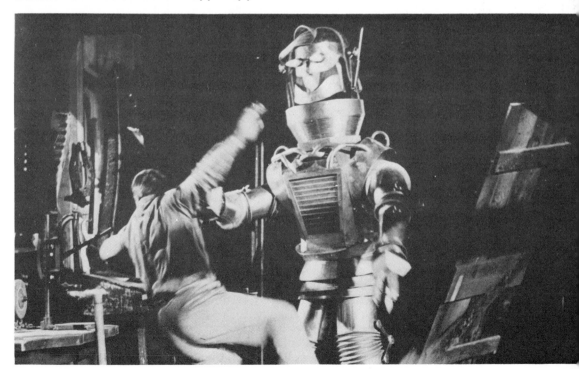

The robot Robby and the boy meet the evil super-computer in *The Invisible Boy* (1957).

aerial invaders were only flying men in their far-out costumes because of the low budgets of the serials. The lack of a decent budget also made *Invaders from Mars* control people electronically — the cheapest way of making robots on screen was to make people act as robots after being taken over by alien infleunces (*See Colour Section)*

Bigger budgets, though, meant realler robots. They were split in their nature, as man is split himself, between good and evil. In that remarkable allegory, *The Day the Earth Stood Still*, Michael Rennie was a visitor from space with the best of intentions — he wanted to make the earth stop the nuclear armaments race, Even if his guardian robot could outface armies and melt tanks with its ray, yet it aimed to preserve peace on earth and bring goodwill to all men. Only when its

master was jailed did it break into his prison cell to rescue him. The robot was lawless only when the good was threatened.

Tobor the Great was about a robot with emotions like the loving robot couple at the end of *R.U.R.* It was also capable of receiving telepathic impulses from people and the stars. So fond was it of its inventor and his grandson that it saved them from spies who kidnapped them for their secrets. In *The Invisible Boy*, another version of Robby the Robot was assembled by a boy at home. It battled an evil super-computer that wanted to rule the world. Briefly, the computer changed Robby from good to evil and sent Robby into the attack against the army; but good triumphed in the end. In fact, the boy himself became invisible for so short a time that the title seemed rather a cheat. More invisible was the benign alien from a space-ship, which cured a crippled

Robby advances against the military.

The robot sneers as it attacks in *The Phantom Creeps* (1939).

A fighting plane sights an alien spaceship in *Earth vs. Flying Saucers* (1956).

boy in *The Cosmic Man* — a sort of galactic faith-healer. *(See Colour Section)*

Other robots were frightening and evil. In the early serial, *The Phantom Creeps*, the robot was as much a gargoyle as a machine. In *Earth vs. Flying Saucers*, the robot invaders arrived in their interstellar frisbees, which are the daily sightings of some modern visionaries. When they came out of their saucers, the robots were not too terrifying and soon fell down like a heap of tin cans. In *Target Earth*, the robots from Venus were far more frightening with crab-like pincers and a death-ray projector working from their heads. Once their metal grip got a girl by the throat in an ultimate garotte, there was little escape for her. Luckily for earth, human scientists fought back and won against the Venusian monsters.

Alien robot intruders from outer space became a very popular screen product. In *Phantom from Space*, an invisible humanoid came down to earth, a threatening nothingness inside his curious pronged space helmet. In *The Earth Dies Screaming*, hordes of robots from the stratosphere assaulted humanity and killed most of mankind. As in *Invisisble Invaders*, the film used the cheap theme of the undead, for the corpses of dead people were resurrected by thought control to act as slaves for the aliens. In *The Mysterians*, the robots seemed to be modelled on the Tin Man from the *Wizard of Oz*, more foolish than fearsome. This Japanese feature even included a robot plot to mate with earth women, surely the furthest make-believe of the machine entering the flesh. *(See Colour Section)*

Sometimes the reverse was true. The *Devil Girl from Mars* came to earth with her deadly robot in search of men for her breeding purposes. The poster made her look so beautiful that she seemed to have no need for extra-terrestial assistance to get men into an embrace with her. *(See Colour Section)* Her robot helper was again a little disappointing in the terror stakes, nothing like as gigantic as *Kronos*, actually the biggest and best of the giant robots. It looked like a couple of vast sugar-cubes on stilts, and it rode

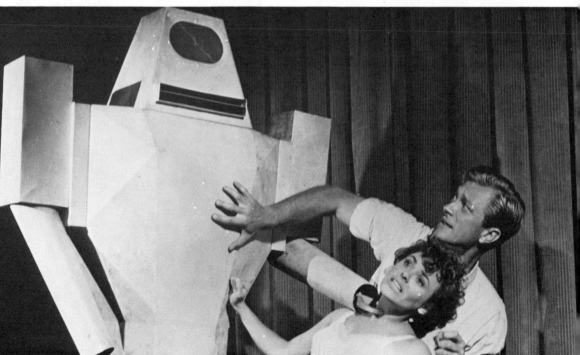

The robot gets a grip on the girl in *Target Earth* (1954).

PHANTOM FROM SPACE

man
or
monster?

WHAT was he?

WHY had he come?

WHO on earth could stop his awesome power, his unguessable desires...his invisible menace?

"PHANTOM FROM SPACE"
Produced and Directed by W. Lee Wilder
Screenplay by Bill Raynor and Myles Wilder
Released Thru United Artists

WHO...OR WHAT WERE THEY?

Be There When **THE EARTH DIES SCREAMING**

STARRING WILLARD **PARKER** • VIRGINIA **FIELD** • DENNIS **PRICE**

PRODUCED BY
ROBERT L. LIPPERT and JACK PARSONS • DIRECTED BY TERENCE FISHER
WRITTEN BY
HENRY CROSS   A LIPPERT FILMS LTD. PRODUCTION
RELEASED BY 20TH CENTURY-FOX

The giant robot leader of *The Mysterians* (1957) amiably pursues the fleeing Japanese.

Dr Jerkoff's space rocket, ready for blast off.

over cities like a hovercraft, sucking up energy through its hollow legs. It both burned and crushed people, and generally it could look a skyscraper in the eye. It was altogether the gargantua of the robots, far superior to the hordes of Daleks buzzing like mechanical bees round Dr Who. *(See Colour Section)* Their invasion of the earth always looked more like dodg'em cars than cosmic crisis.

The funniest of the space robots were undoubtedly the abominable Rapist Robots from planet Porno in the take-off movie *Flesh Gordon*. When they ad-

The Rapist Robots advance at the ready in *Flesh Gordon* (1975).

vanced on the space travellers with their corkscrews palpitating from their crotches, they seemed invincible and penetrating. But they were defeated and the travellers escaped back to Dr Jerkoff's strangely-shaped space rocket and planet Earth, with Dale Ardor breathing, 'There's no place like home!' If the fear of machines taking over mankind remains a real one, at least it can still be exorcised by laughter.

The cosmic monster

All film monsters are robots to some degree, whatever their outer skin. The legendary dragon which attacked Siegfried in Fritz Lang's version of the Nibelung saga was one of the first mechanical beasts to lurch across the screen on wheels and open his mighty jaws. The design of such early robots looked more like coal-mining than computer making; but at least, they worked. The end result was mighty and fearsome, and Siegfied was savaged most satisfactorily by the dragon. Such a nightmare bite has proved one of the primary fears of mankind, culminating in the incredible success of the robot-shark in *Jaws*. Its

The UFA studio design for the dragon in *Siegfried* (1922).

lunge from the deep at the naked lady swimming on the surface has made more money than any film in history.

In between the fifty years between *Siegfried* and *Jaws*, a host of mechanical monsters have stalked the screen, often looking like the animated fantasies of Hieronymous Bosch. They ranged from gigantic insects to mannish deformations to foetal abortions. *The Monster from Green Hell* was more crab than colossus, even if he was an Unstoppable Horror. *The Deadly Mantis* was an overgrown example of his species, treating cars like flies in his murderous advance. Even more atavistic were the visions of gillmen inside scaly suits, for once mankind had crawled out of the sea, or of tree-men attacking from the branches of bushes,

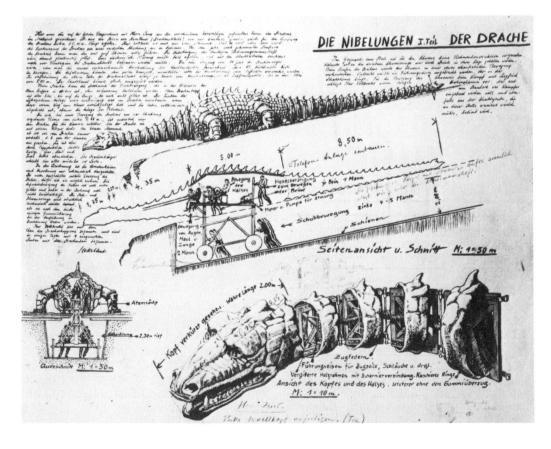

MONSTER from GREEN HELL
Starring JIM DAVIS · BARBARA TURNER · ROBERT E. GRIFFIN

MONSTER from GREEN HELL
Starring JIM DAVIS · BARBARA TURNER · ROBERT E. GRIFFIN

Above: The Deadly Mantis (1957) causes a traffic problem. *Below:* The gill-man grabs the girl in *Revenge of the Creature* (1954).

One of the space monsters looks diabolical . . . And one looks like a deformed man in *Duel of the Space Monsters* (1965).

Corman's mutant carries off the maiden in *The Day the World Ended* (1956).

for once mankind had worshipped trees. The robots of the monster movies could plumb the depths of the fairy tale and the psyche.

More man-size were the deformed creatures in the early Corman low-budget space films, such as the three-eyed, telepathetic cannibal fellows of *The Day the World Ended* or the split-bodied scientist of *War of the Satellites*. (See *Colour Section)* The addition of a few prongs and a rubberised body made mutants out of men. Space monsters, indeed, seemed to have as much to do with the Frankenstein strain as cosmic influences. In *Duel of the Space Monsters,* one of them might as well have come out of the laboratory of a mad earth scientist, even if the others seemed to be dredged up from the depths of an alien hell. The film was actually retitled in

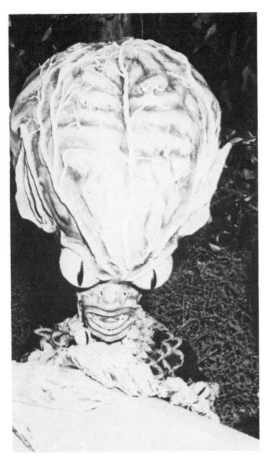 

Left: The aliens plot the destruction of mankind in *Invasion of the Hell Creatures* (1957). *Right:* The Mutant from *This World Earth* (1954).

foreign countries as *Frankenstein Meets the Spacemonster* or *Mars Invades Puerto Rico.*

Yet more interesting were the foetal aliens from outer space with exposed and gigantic brains. The beings in *Invasion of the Hell Creatures* were bulging out all over with grey matter, quite enough to overawe the silly and lesser minds of men. Finally, these little green aliens were illuminated to death by the burning headlights of massed hot-rod cars. They were scaring, but not as scaring as the slave Mutants from Metaluna in *This Island Earth.* These were half-insect and half-human. They also bulged with brains and were able to use red disintegration rays. There was something deeply disturbing in the shapes of these screen creatures, especially for women, as if we could give birth ourselves to foetal monstrosities that might take us over.

In the end, however, the most satisfactory of the robot movie monsters was a mechanical replica created to defeat another movie gargantua. In the fantasist Japanese film, *King Kong Escapes*, the mighty ape found himself confronted with his metal other self. In the horrendous battles between atavistic and electronic apes, mere brontesauri and neanderthal monsters took a terrible drubbing. Yet justice was done. Even the burning rays of the robot Kong could not destroy the rearing flesh of the largest man-monkey of them all. Once again, blood beat metal in the morality play that is the true monster movie.

Future fear

If one of the first dreams of man was to make himself, one of his future fears is that he may unmake himself. All very well to make machines which are obedient, until we become obedient to our very own machines. Charlie Chaplin, always the little man facing the big world, devoted a whole film to taking on the mighty machine — and losing to it. He might be blithe about trying to master the cogs and levers of the factory in *Modern Times*, but finally, the machine chewed him up and swallowed him and excreted him like a titbit, just to prove its supremacy.

Quite literally in science fiction films, the fear of being dwarfed by the machine has led to Lilliputian feelings. In *Dr Cyclops,* for instance, the mechanism for shrinking human beings into slave dolls was a radium canister kept down an old mineshaft. Once miniaturised, the humans were no more than fleas hopping about beneath the pincers of terrible and gigantic instruments. If we have used machines to conduct experiments, cannot we ourselves become the subjects of experiments by the machines? That terror is expressed at its most extreme in the James Bond fantasy *Goldfinger.* In

Below: Charles Chaplin is briefly master of the machine — but not when it starts again. *Right:* Charles Chaplin is not showing off his muscles, but pulling twin levers in *Modern Times* (1936).

Albert Dekker as *Dr Cyclops* (1939) examines his radium canister for miniaturizing people.

that extravaganza, the hero is threatened with emasculation by a giant laser beam, the ultimate threat and triumph of mechanical rape against male pride.

The ancient warrior Spartans used to live in fear of the revolt of their Helot serfs, for the Helots immensely outnumbered them. We are dependent on the Helot machines we have made, and our screen fantasies reflect our fears of a robot revolt. Even the motor car, so much the slave of our leisure and our appetites,

may fight back. In the recent Roger Corman success, *Death Race 2000,* Frankenstein is resurrected behind the wheel of his killer car, The Monster. He aims to kill the maximum number of pedestrians and reach the finish before his rivals — Calamity Jane Kelly in her Stud Bull car, Mathilda the Hun Morris in her Buzz Bomb, Nero Lonigan in The Lion, and Machine Gun Joe in the Peacemaker.

Frankenstein is masked in black because of three near-fatal accidents already — his body is a walking miracle of surgery and scarcely his. But in this latest resurrection, he represents the terror of death by car crash more than the

Above: The tweezers of Dr Cyclops threaten the little man. *Below:* Sean Connery faces the castrating laser beam in *Goldfinger* (1964).

Above and below: Two of the killer cars with their crews in *Death Race 2000.*
Right: David Carradine plays the new Frankenstein in his death car — the
survivor through surgery of three bad crashes.

Above: The hot-rod has its points in *The Cars That Ate Paris* (1975). *Below:* The hot-rod also has jaws in the same film.

COSMIC FRANKENSTEIN TERRORIZES EARTH!

SEE terror sweep through the heart of a city in the dead of night!

THE MAGNETIC MONSTER

IVAN TORS presents
"THE MAGNETIC MONSTER" starring RICHARD CARLSON
featuring King Donovan · Jean Byron · Jarma Lewis · Screenplay by Curt Siodmak
and Ivan Tors · Produced by IVAN TORS · Directed by CURT SIODMAK
An A-Men Production · Released thru United Artists

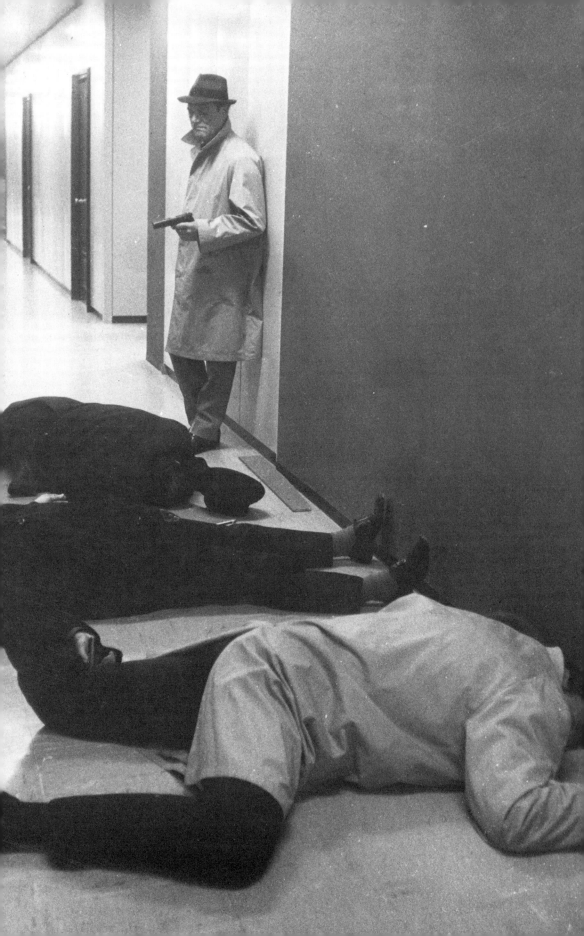

nightmare of monster attack.

An underground classic took the fear of the automobile to its final conclusion. In *The Cars That Ate Paris,* the youths of the little town of Paris set up accidents to steal the parts of the wrecked cars of visitors for their hot-rods. They construct fearsome spiked monsters of racers, more deadly than the mailed fists of the old armoured knights. Then they attack their own town and destroy it with their avenging cars. The last jaws of all are radiator grilles, with metal teeth more engulfing than any white shark's.

This future fear is of a world that out-of-control machines may control. In *The Magnetic Man,* it is an isotope that breeds a robot, which in its turn terrorizes the earth — hardly the 'cosmic Frankenstein' of its poster, yet reflecting a real fear of atomic contamination. In Godard's *Alphaville,* an evil computer controls the whole of mankind, until Lemmy Caution shoots it with his little gun and suddenly every human being is unprogrammed and unalive. In *The Avengers,* Diana Rigg tried to fight off

Left: All die when Lemmy Caution kills the controlling computer mind in *Alphaville* (1965). *Above:* Diana Rigg chops and chops at the karate robot played by Christopher Lee in *The Avengers* (1965).

Christopher Lee, playing a karate robot, and she did so — which was not the case in *Westworld,* where Yul Brynner played the rebellious robot gunman going beserk and hunting down all the holiday-makers, who had expected to shoot him down for a thrill in that computerized and robot-staffed vacationland. In his remorseless and murderous advance, Brynner managed to show the terror of the implacable robot better then any actor since the late Boris Karloff.

Yet two recent films made the Hephaestus strain and the Frankenstein strain seem very near the here and now. One was *THX 1138,* in which computers and robot policemen mastermind a drugged population in an underground city. A girl cuts off the hero's drug supply, which has acted like the traditional

The robot gunman threatens the holiday-maker in *Westworld* (1973).

bromide in the soldier's tea and has stopped him thinking of sex. He falls in love with her, she is killed by the robots, he escapes to the sunlight and the surface of the earth. In the machine, destruction. In escape to nature, release.

More timely, more terrifying was that underrated classic of science fiction, *Soylent Green.* It saw the last performance of that great actor, Edward G. Robinson. He played an aged scholar, who discovered the secret of the last processed food of mankind before voluntarily choosing euthanasia. His discovery was that mankind was so packed on the surface of the earth that it was eating its own processed bodies to stay alive. The proper study of mankind was no longer man, but the terminal diet of mankind was man.

In *Soylent Green,* the Malthusian nightmare of an overpopulated world of city mobs, controlled by a few men using machines to scoop up any dissidents like a spoon scoops up grits, is the final solution. Man not only makes too many machines to serve and dominate himself. He also breeds too many replacements for himself. Billions of babies, as *R.U.R.* pointed out, are more inefficient than billions of robots, and they cost far more — perhaps even the price of life on earth. In fact, the explosion of the machine is only because of the need to feed and clothe and house exploding humanity.

Once we were told to multiply and replenish the earth. We have done so, and we find that we are multiplying and replenishing the garbage-bins. Yes, we are Hephaestus, we are Prometheus, we are Frankenstein. We can make all the machines we want, and we can make more mankind than we do want. But if we make too many of both robots and replacements for ourselves, we will become robots of the flesh — forced to live like regimented ants just to survive.

The drugged population goes about its work in the underground city in *THX 1138* (1969).

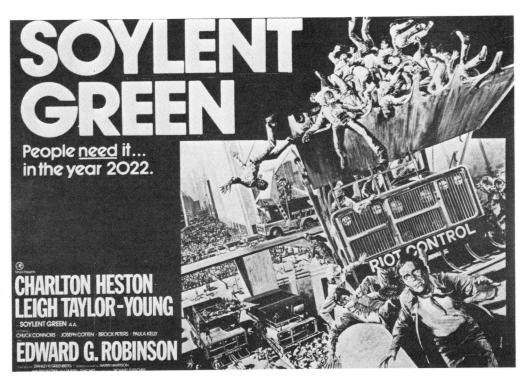

Charlton Heston gets swept down the conveyor belt of the protein packs made from dead people in *Soylent Green* (1973).